The
old Medal
Mindset

eps to Achieve Success
om an Olympic Trainer
and Many Great Masters

Printed in the United States of America

ISBN 978-1-5197-8710-1

www.FitnessHope.com

DEDICATION

to dedicate this book to my loving family, friends who
ne and the many masters who inspired me, and to all
s who have trusted me to inspire them.

Contents

5

Preface

When writing this book, I was inspire
spread this message and the techniques of
"Gold Medal Mindset" to make a difference
same way it did for me, my children, and th
thousands of people I've had the pleasure c
coaching. Born in Greece, I was an athlete r
discus, track and field, volleyball, soccer, ba
and many other sports. I participated in Wc
in 1994, carrying the banner for my home c
Pasadena.

;covered a passion for coaching and for
/enty-five years I have coached people to
h their ideal health and fitness goals.
ny clients have won world championships,
ipionships, and Olympic medals. Both of
en are NCAA champions. However, the
·f people I helped were average people
ed to achieve an ideal healthy body. I am
ɔ make a difference in your life in the way
·rs and teachers have made a difference in
e will break it down into three simple
dset, practice, and inspiration. With these
will be able to live your ideal life in
your health, love and joy.

don't need to be a professional athlete to
e same results! The results that all those
ny children achieved are something you
ence in your own life.

My daughter Athena with her NCAA volleyball champ
and son Apollo with his NCAA football champions

About Me

as born in Athens, Greece in a one-room
h four children and no kitchen or
. My father was illiterate and I and had to
 to write his own signature. My parent's
 was to earn money in order to survive
he family. I was always the dreamer. My
me from going to school and listening to
out Hercules, Jason and the Golden
d all the other great mythological stories.
ed my imagination and gave wings to my
aduated from the University of Athens,
y PhD in Los Angeles and I am healthy with
omes. There are no excuses, no matter
 upbringing or background. Growing up in
owing up was one of the greatest
es of my life. It propelled me and showed
y. My motto was get the best education
 matter what the problem, there is always
 and everything will work out.

children, my clients, and I have
hed what we set our minds to. You don't

need to win a gold medal, win a champion: live in million dollar homes to have a mind success. Living your ideal life, full of joy an your terms is your gold medal in life. I than many great masters who have helped teac mindset for mastery including Socrates, Ein Ghandi, Aristotle, Thoreau, Abraham Linco Picasso, Eleanor Roosevelt, Winston Churc Jesus, and many others.

The main problem people face is tha are listening to their internal chatter and ig the reality that has served them very well. getting stuck in the negative frame of minc cannot study and live in the ideal place of l love and joy like the great masters did.

My solution is to give you the minds by using a practical step-by-step process, e me, my family and my clients to achieve th mindset of the great masters. This Gold M Mindset has helped my clients, my childre to create success—and it will help you too

Think Like An Olympian

hink like an Olympian, you must get into
et of thinking like a creator, not a Copy
This is the main focus of people that
ings that have never been achieved
r example, an athlete breaking the four-
le was once thought of as impossible, but
epted and has been done many times.

py Machine is someone who constantly
hat has been said and done by other
you listen to the news on TV, the same
nstantly repeated on different channels.
o them, you focus on what someone else
 instead of thinking about your own ideas
hts. A common story people copy is about
ce caps melting. They have not verified it
s; they just repeat the story. Currently we
ice forming on the planet. If you search
d out the caps forming on both poles
 below the water. Ice melts and reforms
e and is a common occurrence on this
e mindset is what takes you to a negative

or positive case scenario. More than 90 pe
the fears people have never materialize or
They say things like "I cannot do that," "I ca
lose the weight," "I can't drop my blood pr
without medication," "I cannot raise my er
natural way without stimulants." My exper
with all of my clients is that they can achie
they believe is impossible.

The mindset of a Creator is focused
ideal case scenario, or the "dream come tr
example, consider the case of Thomas Edis
People thought he failed three thousand ti
have a working light bulb. But his mindset
he knew was he knew three thousand filar
that would not work in a light bulb. He per
and achieved his goal; light bulbs are now
common household necessity.

Another example is Walt Disney. He
little pad of paper with a drawing of a mou
was trying to convince people about his dr
People thought that little mouse on a piec
would never work, but look at it now! He c

g that now gives joy and pleasure to
people on this planet. Walt Disney had
set of mastery.

e the example of the basketball greats,
ordan and Magic Johnson. They both won
als in the Olympic Games. By taking that
nto the rest of their life both of them are
chy billionaires while the vast majority of
her teammates are now scraping to get by.
ordan and Magic Johnson were creative
who transferred their wealth and money
eal estate industry. They bought sports
d invested in living like creators. They took
from basketball into business, and family

ualizing is a very important tool to put you
idset of mastery to accomplish your goals.
your ideal case scenario, feel it vividly out
tom of your body and feel how it actually
–the joy and happiness. Visualizing is a
practice. Without it you will not reach a
hindset. With it you will achieve this

mindset and excel. You have to play out you
case with strong feelings, seeing in your mi
that it is done and how happy you are.

The famous American Indian athlete
Thorpe was traveling by boat to Germany v
US Olympic team. Every athlete was on the
working out while Thorpe was sitting on a c
his eyes closed. When asked by his coach v
wasn't training, he said "I am training, Coac
repeating every step and move I will be doi
left with multiple gold medals, defeating Hi
statement proclaiming that only white Gerr
would win medals since the Aryan race was
superior race. He attributed his visual and r
practice to his success.

It is all about the euphoric feeling. W
are in the Gold Medal Mindset, you feel tha
are flying high. You are lucky, healthy, and
When you are having fears and doubts you
obviously out of the right mindset. You star
blaming other people rather than looking a
yourself. You are the only one in charge an

f your destiny. The moment you start
ing you are out of the right mindset. When
ou are the creator, in charge and
g is going right, you are in the right
It's like when you are riding on a train.
u realize you are going the wrong
, you can't just instantly start going in the
direction. It's not feasible for the contents
in. You slow down the train, then stop,
ly reverse until you gain speed going the
irection again. Your thoughts work the
. You slow down the thoughts that don't
ortable, stop in the present, and reverse
ositive mindset of mastery.

eighty-seven-year-old grandmother, Vicky,
back and hip by slipping on a step.
n the hospital for three months and things
ing worse and worse. After I consulted
reminding her of what she achieved in her
ly and her strong beliefs, she was able to
nind on. By making some small
nts to her health, she was able to turn her
the Gold Medal mindset. Without an

15

operation, just a brace and her will she's no
to walk without a cane and swim—when b
was headed into the grave.

Vicky: From broken back to cane-free walking

Cathy, a client, came to me asking to
her marathon running. At the time, she wa
a fifteen-minute mile. Within the first two
she was able reduce her time to eleven mir
mile, but she realized she was having a bloc
pressure problem. Through working on her
exercise and diet we were able to drop her
pressure down from 157 with medication t
without medication.

fifty-eight, Francisco was left disabled after
h. Before he started training with me, his
nergy was three out of ten when he woke
e day. Now he wakes up at a seven or eight
s it throughout the day. The mind was his
lock but with mental training coupled with
exercise, we were able to bring him to his
partan status.

e mindset of a Creator is wonderfully
ed in one of the great masters, Jesus.
us was told Lazarus was dead and a giant
s closing his grave, he ignored the others
llowed his mindset of mastery. He went up
ne and said, "Lazarus, come out!" and
se from the dead.

ou want to be successful in your life and
t health, love, and joy, think the way the
ters and Olympians thought. Follow the
will outline for you and practice what has
cticed by the great masters. Become a
ot a copy machine, and you will be happy.

Mindset

In order to accomplish your goals, you mindset has to stay focused on your ideal so You must have the right momentum and be with your ideal goals. Those are the ingredie the mindset of an Olympian master. There i of momentum. When you focus for over 16 on a particular subject, it creates momentu you do this for over a minute it's very hard that momentum. It's important to be aware where your momentum is aligned. It can ali spiral upward towards your ideal goal or ali spiral downward where everything goes wr

Focus

Looking at the chart below there are 6 places where your mind can focus. Positive future, negative future, positive present, negative present, positive past, and negative past. You have to determine where you are.

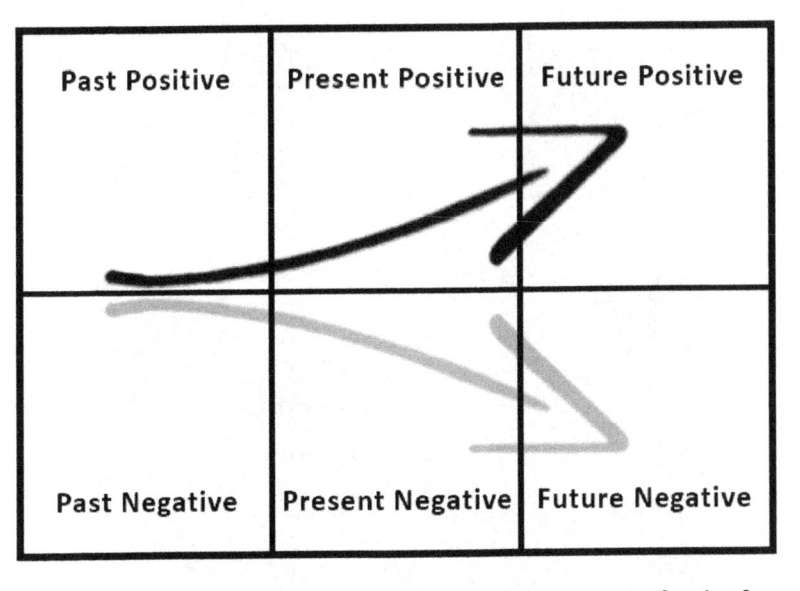

Past Positive	Present Positive	Future Positive
Past Negative	Present Negative	Future Negative

The easiest way is to look at how you feel. If you are optimistic and happy, you are most likely on the positive side. If you feel unlucky, or that things aren't going right for you, you are on the negative side. The goal is to focus on the positive present and project the ideal scenario. Count your blessings: your family, home, health, or whatever you can positively identify with. Be aware of the internal chatter, the thoughts running through your mind, and feelings in your body. If you are thinking about being on the podium and on the gold medal, you are on the right track. If you are worried about paying rent, you are on the wrong track. If you feel happy and joyful, you are on the right track. If you are pessimistic and worrying, you are on the wrong track. The goal is for you to focus on your ideal future.

Some ideas of negative thoughts are: *I'm not sure I can do it, I'm not sure of that, I don't know if it can be done.* This is the verbalization of those who are on the negative side. Consider those statements versus *Yes, I can, Yes, I will, It has been done before, Others have done it, I've done it before.* Be a guided missile of finding current things I am thankful for no matter how little they are. Seek out for any little positives, things to be thankful for or appreciative of from having a place to sleep, having friends, to being alive.

Momentum

What you focus on grows. Take this example of a Thanksgiving family dinner. Some people began a conversation about the economy declining. The next person brought up a grimmer subject about violence in the world is getting worse and worse, then then another person talked about the ice caps melting and how the planet is being destroyed. This spiraled a beautiful Thanksgiving dinner into chaos. You have to be aware of the law of momentum. When you participate, the movement gets worse and worse. When it goes on more than a minute, it gets completely out of control.

If you want to understand momentum, imagine a stroller carrying your child on the top of a steep hill. If it rolls a few inches, it is very easy to stop. If you let the stroller roll a few feet, it gets harder and harder to catch up to stop it. If it goes twenty to thirty feet down the hill, it becomes dangerous to catch and stop it and could be disastrous.

The law of momentum is a steep downward hill. If you let go, gravity will take over and disaster will follow. The only place to take control is in the very beginning; once you let things go, they will be beyond control within a minute. Ideally, catch yourself within the first sixteen seconds. Realize this and learn that you can stop and reverse the moment to align it to where you want to go. This way you can accomplish your ideal goals of health, love, and fun.

When your mindset is going upwards, and you're thinking the right way, you are thinking like an Olympian. You feel lucky, as though the universe is conspiring in your favor. You feel like you're driving and every light is green. Friends are calling and offering little assistances to help you get where you are going. Lucky random coincidences are common for you and happiness and joy is the outcome.

Momentum takes about sixteen seconds to start having an effect in the direction you are going. After four cycles of this or one minute it becomes a strong force whose direction is difficult to control. The first sixteen seconds it builds up, the next sixteen seconds doubles the force, the next quadruples and the next sixteen seconds makes the momentum sixty-four times stronger. The consequences of this can be amazing (like a gold medal) or disastrous depending on the direction of your momentum. This is in your thoughts, spoken words, conversation, and everything around us. Our intention of where to focus our attention is very critical. It's a good idea to choose to plant a seed of a positive thought or subject of conversation. After sixteen seconds of conversation, you start a spiral forward. Then if you have company, others will join you and will gain more positive force. This builds a magnetic field of attraction that attracts positive thoughts and feelings; it feels like getting lucky.

Alignment

Alignment is important when you want to be on the same level as your goals, intentions, and ideal case life scenario. If you want to accomplish a gold medal in the Olympic Games or other health and financial goals, it's a good ideal to think, talk, associate and expose yourself in that direction. You don't want to go the wrong way and talk about what you don't want; only talk about the good experiences that you will have when you achieve your best case scenario. Let's assume finance is your goal and you want to make a million dollars. Begin to talk about how it feels to have a million dollars and what you would do with it. Watch movies or TV shows about people winning a million dollars. You want to eat, sleep, and think it. You don't want to think about the lack of money and your obstacles to obtaining it. You'll create the wrong momentum backwards instead of downward.

If you go the wrong way, you'll know because you don't feel good. We all have an internal guidance system to know if we don't feel good or if something doesn't feel right. It might be in your head or body or stomach; it's a feeling you have to be aware of. If you go the right way you feel good, optimistic, and lucky. People are nice to you when you drive. You are a magnet of positive things instead of negative ones. This is why you want to keep your focus in alignment with your ideal case scenario.

Imagine a train going northbound from Los Angeles to San Francisco. If the train is going the wrong way 100mph it can't just suddenly turn around and go 100 mph. The contents of the train could suffer badly. You want to slow down the train gently and eventually stop then go slowly the other way. The way we do this in the mindset is using a breathing technique. You want to use a thought pattern interruption. To do this, you stop thinking, dwelling, and talking about the subject that is going the wrong way. The way you do this is by utilizing your breath. You can silently say *breathe in...* *breathe out...*as you count your breaths. You can enhance the thought pattern interruption with visualizations. The brain cannot think two things at the same time so we interrupt the thought pattern. Then we can control your thoughts to begin a seed of a positive thought pattern that will amplify into your ideal life goal.

Practice

There is a technique that has worked for the great masters and great Olympians. They first had a vision of their success; this is the most important thing. The best time to practice is before we get out of bed and before we go to sleep at night. During this time our minds are in between beta and alpha brain waves where our unconscious is most likely to take suggestions. This is when you want to visualize your ideal case scenario. Imagine it's like a YouTube video. Visualize a movie with the perfect outcome. Maybe it's a movie of you on a podium winning a gold medal. Maybe it's you cashing a check or standing at the altar. See it vividly like a little movie. If your mind goes anywhere else, go into your breath.

How to Visualize

Be in a comfortable, quiet place without distractions. Just before you go to sleep or just after waking up are good times. Make sure that the temperature is good and there is no ambient noise.

To quiet your mind, focus your attention on your breath. Start slowing your mind down. Say (either internally or out loud) "breathe in" and "breathe out." If you need a stronger focus, start counting, "Breathe in one, breathe out one." If you want to enhance this, picture a baby angel coming and writing a number one on your heart, then erasing the number and writing a two with your next breath. Keep going to nine breaths in/out until you're ready to start your visualization.

Your ideal case scenario starts. Try to see yourself with as much detail as you can happily accomplishing your ideal goal. How does it feel physically when you live your ideal goal? Where are you? What are you doing? Who is around you? Who congratulates or embraces you? What are your specific accomplishments?

Make sure that you enhance the visualization with emotions and feelings of joy. Magnify the visualization with the emotion. You want to feel the joy, feel it on your skin, feel it on every cell in your body. Feel the celebration of everybody else around you. Smell the air and magnify the surroundings of your vision.

When going through the visualization, be thankful as if your goal has already been accomplished. Imagine you're giving your Oscar acceptance speech, thanking everyone around you and the people who got you there. See them happy and give them credit. You might thank your parents, your friends, God, or whoever is important to you.

If your mind starts to wander to another place, go back to Step Two and repeat in the same order.

Try to do at least two to three minutes at a time, up to fifteen minutes. The longer you practice, the better results you'll have.

When finished with your visualization, focus on your breathing again, counting down from nine to one.

My Ideal Visualization Scenario

My own meditation I start in the morning before I get out of bed. I lay comfortably under my covers and my eyes are closed. I turn on my iPhone meditation to music that puts me into the right mood. I focus on my breathing and when I inhale I see a little baby angel. On the shape of heart, he writes the number "one" and when I exhale another smiling baby angel erases the number one. When I inhale the second time, another baby angel comes and writes the number "two" and this repeats till the number nine. This prepares my mind and quiets it. If there were any thoughts about what time it is and what I have to do, I clear my mind completely by focusing on my breathing. Then I start visualizing a beautiful movie of my life.

I visualize being a director of a wellness center in the rainforest making a difference in people's lives. I am educating them with the live blood cell analysis, explaining the benefits of detoxification, listening to their goals, and writing and outlining a program for them. Then I see them at the end, happy and radiant and smiling and hugging me. I amplify the vision with emotion and even tears of joy. I imagine smiles and hugs; I imagine joy. I feel a tingling sensation on my skin like my hair standing up. I feel wellness, a sense of wellbeing. We both give thanks to each other, feeling fulfilled. I say that I'm thankful for all the experiences in my life. I'm so appreciative for every single thing that happened in my life, even some of them that temporarily didn't look or feel good. They were very important lessons that guided me to be where I am. So I am thankful now for my hardships and my hard work; they were great teachers for me. I appreciate those temporary hard times and realize now what a gift they were. I wish the same thing for everyone—all of all the beautiful people that are all around me—that they will be able to touch other's lives the same way my life was touched.

To leave the visualization, I do the breathing the other way around. I count from angel number nine to angel number one. When the visualization is finished, I am joyful, alive, and having a great day.

Visualizing a Staircase

I imagine that in order to reach the gold medal, deposit the million dollar check into my account or whatever goal you have, there is a staircase. At the top is the vault, the bank, the medal; your ideal case scenario. When I am comfortable in my bed doing my visualization exercises and after I do my exercises I go to the next step of the ladder where I visualize my day starting and doing all the necessary physical requirements towards that goal. It's like looking at my dream card with all my goals written down. Then I see myself going up to the third step and I appreciate my day so far before I started my visualization. I give thanks and then I go up to the next step, where I make sure that physically my body is rested and in a good health or fitness level to keep going. Then I go to the next step, when I smile and I say thank you for all the cooperative people in my life: my parents, teachers, friends, and family. On the next step, I emotionally intensify how good it feels with my goal accomplished. I imagine the joy I feel, the environment around whether it's in a bank or at an Olympic Games. Then I go the next step up, where I have all those wonderful people congratulating, thanking, and enjoying being with me, taking pictures with me and taking autographs. I take the next step up the spiral and see myself lecturing and teaching on how I accomplished my goals. I give them hope and direction and see myself teaching them how powerful they are. I tell them how they will do more than I did, how they will solve problems that my generation couldn't, and see them laughing, happy and gaining power. I go to the next step and I see a beautiful appreciation gathering with ballroom dancing. Elderly people gather and appreciate me. Then I see my family. They are happily appreciating and hugging me. I am giving away money and my awards. I imagine the joy they receive when they get the money because they are a part of the whole thing.

Sometimes I do these visualizations three to five times a day and sometimes I do them every three to five days.

There is a simple method to help you understand your negative thoughts and move past them into a positive mindset. An example is shown on the next page:

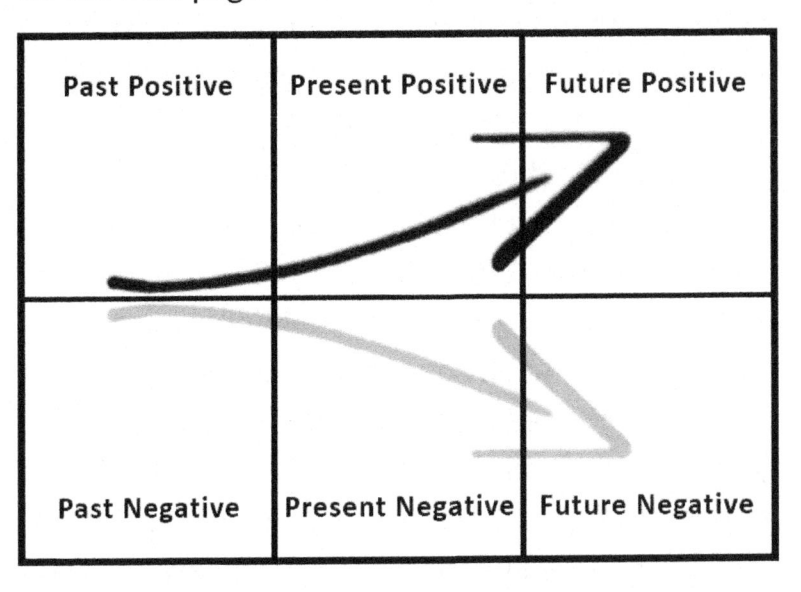

Past Positive	Present Positive	Future Positive
Past Negative	Present Negative	Future Negative

You can draw this diagram on an 8.5x11 sheet of paper.

Six blocks represent the past, present and future. It's easiest to start from past. Write down the negative thoughts you are having about the past. If you feel stuck in negative thought, use the breathing exercise and breathe through the negative thoughts until the weight feels lifted off. Just focus on feeling your breathe until the negative moment is stopped. Move into your Present then into your Future thinking about your negative thoughts or worries. Repeat the breathing exercises until the negative moment is over. Then move to the next row and write down thoughts from the Past that make you appreciative or happy. Move to the Present, then to what you are looking forward to in the future. The Positive side of this diagram is what you should keep your focus on. Go to your breathing exercise so you can stop negative momentum.

Stay in the present positive and try to visualize between the present positive and the future positive, drawing experience from the past if it helps you. But not everyone has that experience if it is appropriate to draw from the positive past. Otherwise visualize the appreciation which is the positive past.

For more inspirational quotes, tips and training, sign up at

www.FitnessHope.com

Inspirational Messages

Over the last 20 years I have been lucky enough to have my own business. I didn't have anyone to motivate me and inspire me so I had to find my own inspiration and motivation. I had a habit every day of searching one of the great masters to start my day with and dwell upon. After I did this for a few months, a client asked if I could email them the motivational quotes. After I emailed it to one person then another then I got into the habit of doing the motivation daily for everyone, including all of my clients and friends now. What influenced me to write this book you're reading now has been inspired by the following masters and it makes a great deal of difference to me, my family, and thousands of clients. My life is a lot better because of all those great masters' quotes and energy.

1.

At least once a day, allow yourself the freedom to think and dream for yourself.

Albert Einstein

1.

Thinking for yourself is a beautiful way to map your life towards your goals. Practicing thinking for yourself instead of regurgitating what others think is an empowering and useful practice to me towards developing the mindset of an Olympian.

2.

A human being always acts and feels and performs in accordance with what he imagines to be true about himself and his Environment.

Maxwell Maltz

2.

When I first came to the US I loved music, but I never went to school. I didn't have an instrument. In my New Year's visualization, I saw myself playing a musical instrument and enjoying it. Within six months a friend came asked me and asked what I wanted. I said "whatever you want," so he brought me a balalaika. I started practicing and within a few months I had a party at my house playing music and we created a pera (a group of friends in Greek). The beauty of it was that for the next twenty-five years I had the pleasure of performing in countless concerts, weddings, parties, and at universities. My visualization, which started in my imagination, brought music into my life and I'm thankful to everyone that was a cooperative component.

3.

If you don't see yourself as a winner, then you cannot perform as a winner.

Zig Ziglar

3.

Focus on what you want to see in your life, not what you DO NOT want to see. Like a magnet, you will attract what is your most dominant thought. That happened to me, my children and most of my clients. It's obvious to me whatever we focus on manifests into our life in the entire spectrum of positive to negative.

4.

I will not let anyone walk through my mind with dirty feet.

Gandhi (1869 - 1948)

4.

We have a choice about which way to go. Our thoughts thus determine our future life. If we think pleasant, positive, uplifting thoughts and have open conversations on that subject, beautiful things will happen. I've seen some of my clients allow negative thoughts to take momentum. Not understanding that power and stopping that moment leads to unpleasant experiences.

5.

Worrying is using your imagination to create something you don't want.

Abraham Hicks

5.

Using imagination the wrong way can have disastrous effects. Imagination in the right way will give you wonderful results. You choose!

6.

Anytime you run into a wall or a closed door, the first place to try to open it is in your own mind.

Source unknown

6.

I was a trained economist working in the oil industry in LA but I wasn't a good fit for the philosophy and the "clique." It didn't feel good. I discovered that my calling was to make a difference in another area, which was people's health, athletic performance and wellness overall. I consider my experience as an economist as a blessing as it was a guidance to what really makes my heart rejoice.

7.

What a man thinks of himself, that it is which determines, or rather indicates, his fate.

Henry David Thoreau (1817 - 1862)

7.

There is a whole philosophy around the "I AM" that is a worthwhile to take a look at. Thoreau is right; what I was determined to be, I became. I am the master of my fate. My upbringing from an illiterate father in a poor environment had nothing to do with my fate. Being a dreamer paid off big time. As a businessman, as a professor, as a mentor, father, doctor and friend I made the choice, not my environment or upbringing.

8.

The energy of the mind is the essence of life.

Aristotle (384 - 322 BC)

8.

Your thoughts are so powerful; it's like food. When you eat good food, you are healthy, strong, and vibrant. If you eat bad food, your body, health and wealth might not become as powerful.

9.

Always bear in mind that your own resolution to succeed is more important than any other one thing.

Abraham Lincoln

9.

It is important to be the creator of your life. Take control of your thoughts and mindset so you can accomplish exactly what you are aiming for. Nobody else will do that for you.

10.

We would focus on everything that mattered to us. It is so satisfying to hold a thought and to find the feeling place and then see the Universe conspire to help you receive it. Oh, co-creation at its best.

Abraham Hicks

10.

It is so wonderful to concentrate on your ideal case scenario and see all the necessary ingredients come together. It's like magic. When you visualize, you're not the only one visualizing. You're not the only one who wants your success.

11.

The best way to predict the future is to invent it.

Alan Kay, Computer Scientist

11.

Take control so you can go in the right direction and end up where you want to go instead of being taken wherever the wind blows. It's a lot better to determine your future instead of waiting for better things to come to you.

12.

People think I'm disciplined. It is not discipline. It is devotion. There is a great difference."

Luciano Pavarotti Opera Singer

12.

What I do now for a living is my passion. I find myself enjoying twelve to sixteen-hour work days and I want to keep going. It doesn't feel like work; it feels like I'm playing. I make a difference in people's lives, they make a difference in mine and it feels wonderful. There is a huge difference between what doing you love doing versus something that you have to do. Try it—I bet you are going to like it.

13.

The world is but canvas to our imaginations.

Henry David Thoreau

13.

If we can go towards our dreams, we can realize them. Following my dreams allows me the freedom to create and enjoy and make a difference that I choose to determine. It was my choice and nobody else's.

14.

At the touch of love everyone becomes a poet.

Plato (c.427 - 347 BC)

14.

I was lucky enough to fall in love with wellness and sports at an early age. I had the benefit of a wonderful life and experiences from Olympic games, World Cups, and world championships to my children's softball, football, and volleyball games. Love has been the main ingredient and the main reward.

15.

Every time you tell your better-feeling story, you will feel better and the details of your life will improve. The better it gets, the better it gets.

Abraham Hicks

15.

When you visualize, be as specific and elaborate as you can and add to it each time. Keep improving as you go along.

16.

To accomplish great things, we must dream as well as act.

Anatole France

16.

There is an old joke about a very religious person who believed in God strongly. A rainstorm came and the man was stuck on his roof in a flood. A rowboat, a motorboat and a helicopter all passed by him and the people inside offered him help. But the man said "No, God will save me." The man died and in heaven he asked God "Why didn't you save me?" God said "I sent you a rowboat, and motor boat and helicopter; what more did you expect?"

17.

You and I do make the difference,
Begin today and make the difference.

If each of us were to say:
One person does not make the difference,
There would never be love and peace on earth.

If each grain of sand were to say:
One grain does not make a mountain,
There would be no land.

If each drop of water were to say:
One drop does not make an ocean,
There would be no sea.

If each note of music were to say:
Each note does not make a symphony,
There would be no melody.

If each word were to say:
One word does not make a library,
There would be no book.

If each brick were to say:
One brick does not make a wall,
There would be no house.

If each seed were to say:
One seed does not make a field,
There would be no harvest.

Author Unknown

17.
Just do it.

18.

Do, or do not.
There is no try.

Yoda

18.

When you do something, do it with all of your heart until the very end with only the end result in your mind. Magic happens when you surrender all doubt and fears and just go for it.

19.

Imagination will often carry us to worlds that never were. But without it, we go nowhere.

Carl Sagan

19.

Your ability to imagine is your ability to visualize your way into allowing miracles happen.

20.

Whatever you're thinking about is literally like planning a future event.

When you're worrying, you are planning.

When you're appreciating you are planning...

What are you planning?

Abraham Hicks

20.

Your choice of thinking, visualizing, expressing is a wonderful tool. I see it in my life, my family, and my clients. It can work miracles—or nightmares—if you so choose.

21.

First say to yourself what you would be; and then do what you have to do.

Epictetus

21.

Visualize yourself moving step by step into your ideal situation. Do this often and the actions you must take will naturally appear when you need to take them.

22.

I am always doing that which I can not do, in order that I may learn how to do it.

Pablo Picasso

22.

In the past, I never could have imagined that I would perform with accomplished musicians that have performed in Carnegie Hall and concerts all over the world. If I used my lack of training or not having an instrument as reasons to fail, I would have never have been able to perform with them. The beautiful dimension of music came into my life because I could visualize success—even though logically I never could have thought it to come true.

23.

People are just as happy as they make up their minds to be.

Abraham Lincoln

23.

Your goal is what matters, not what society thinks or anyone else's standards. If your goal is to be a happy mother, work on that mission. If your goal is to be an Olympic athlete, then work on that. If your goal is to be a good provider work on that. You choose your life.

24.

Intention is always more powerful than conditions.

Alan Cohen

24.

There is a magic in the power of intention that can overcome any condition. When I tried to come to the USA, I was declined and my passport was stamped "unwelcome". Yet I visualized my ideal outcome, eventually a solution appeared where there was none before and I was allowed back. Who would have guessed the ambassador and I were both discus throwers?

25.

What you do is miniscule in comparison with what you choose to think, because your vibration is so much more powerful and so much more important.

Abraham Hicks

25.

Logic has limitations, but feelings have infinite power. Through visualization, you can use your feelings as a tool to create solutions to problems.

26.

The pessimist sees difficulty in every opportunity. The optimist sees the opportunity in every difficulty.

Winston Churchill

26.

Every moment is a choice to spiral upward or downward. You can choose to see a half empty or a half full glass. What you choose will determine what happens in your life.

27.

I think and think for months and years. Ninety-nine times, the conclusion is false. The hundredth time I am right.

Albert Einstein

27.

Persistence is power. When you focus on a problem in the beginning it may look impossible. But when you keep focusing on the solution, it goes from impossible to looking improbable and eventually with persistence the solution becomes inevitable.

28.

Every man is what he is because of the dominating thoughts which he permits to occupy his mind.

Napoleon Hill

28.

The rays of the sun can start a fire, but without concentration it's just a warm day. When you concentrate your thoughts, there is a beautiful power that can turn a warm ray into a raging fire.

29.

Dreams are the touchstones of our character.

Henry David Thoreau

29.

Dreams are like a preview of the upcoming attraction. They are like a recharging station for your battery. Dreams are who you are and where you belong trying to show themselves to you.

30.

Desire is the beginning of all new Creation.

Abraham Hicks

30.

Imagine that you plant a seed in the ground, fertilize it, give it water, and then expect a beautiful fruit to grow. The way that a farmer plants an apple tree and any other fruit tree and it bears fruit is the same way we start creation. Plant your seeds of desire according to which fruit you want to harvest.

31.

Is it so bad to be misunderstood? Pythagoras was misunderstood, and Socrates, and Jesus, and Luther, and Copernicus, and Galileo, and Newton, and every pure and wise spirit that ever took flesh.

Ralph Waldo Emerson

31.

The good opinion of others around us should be irrelevant to our dreams and goals. Look at Galileo. They were going to burn him alive because they did not believe that the earth was not the center of the solar system. If we wait for everyone to understand us, we will never excel, we will never progress. Progress has sacrifices, but the rewards are amazing.

32.

It takes a long time to become young.

Pablo Picasso

32.

It takes a long time to accumulate wisdom. Take your time to become young in spirit. Take your time to become young in your thoughts. Just enjoy the travels and the experiences. You know the saying that says "Youth is wasted on the young"?

33.

Imagination is everything. It is the preview of life's coming attractions."

Albert Einstein

33.

Knowledge and science include only what we know up to this time, while imagination includes what we will know in the future. Thus, imagination is a lot more important. Going to Mars used to be thought of as impossible and now there are plans to make it a reality.

34.

The quickest way to solve a problem is to not see it as a problem.

Source unknown

34.

Focusing on all possible solutions is the mindset of all achievers. Analyzing the problem gets you stuck in the thought process that created the problem. The way out is to keep focusing on solutions.

35.

Get so fixated on what you want, that you drown out any vibration or reverberation that has anything to do with what you do not want.

Abraham Hicks

35.

Focusing your attention on your goal will bring your desires. It's like navigating from Marina del Rey to Catalina. The compass steers us most of the time off course, but you always adapt and adjust, always focusing on your goal. Even though it may look like you're off course, if you steer in the right direction, you will always end up in Catalina. You'll always end up where you need to go.

36.

Wherever you go, go with all your heart.

Confucius

36.

Concentrate your attention to your task at hand. It will win you the "gold medal" or the goal at hand. Give it your all.

37.

Man is what he believes.

Anton Chekhov

37.

In order to have joy in your life, you need to have faith in yourself. This a lot more important than any circumstances, a lot more important than any obstacles or conditions. Beliefs are the most important ingredient in accomplishing your goals.

38.

Circumstances may cause interruptions and delays, but never lose sight of your goal. Prepare yourself in every way you can by increasing your knowledge and adding to your experience, so that you can make the most of opportunity when it occurs.

Mario Andretti, Auto Racer

38.

Having the right tools to accomplish the task at hand is as important as having an umbrella when it rains, having a heavy coat when it's cold, or using a bathing suit when you go swimming. You must adjust and adapt in order to accomplish the task at hand.

39.

The future belongs to those who see possibilities before they become obvious.

John Sculley, Business Executive

39.

Start with the end in mind and don't worry about the details to begin with. It will reveal itself and fall together like a beautiful puzzle.

40.

It is never too late to become what you might have been.

George Eliot

40.

Never, ever give up on your dreams. It is worth dreaming and trying. The process is wonderful and usually works. Keep it up.

41.

Imagine having the courage to take a risk, play the odds, be the person who invests in the unknown and ends up winning.

Caroline Myss

41.

I left from Greece to Los Angeles not knowing anyone, where I was going to stay or what I was going to eat. It worked out better than I ever imagined.

42.

Success is a self-fulfilling prophecy.

H.H. Swami Tejomayananda

42.

Success is reaffirming that visualization, goal setting, and mental focus. These are the most important ingredients which are all controlled by your thoughts. Together these manifest beautifully into your goals and desires.

43.

Dreams pass into the reality of action. From the actions stems the dream again; and this interdependence produces the highest form of living.

Anais Nin

43.

Having the right mindset and the right plan of action are needed. They act as one; without the right mindset you can't take the right actions. But taking the right actions without the right mindset won't get you results either.

44.

When the bull's-eye becomes as big in your mind as an elephant, you are sure to hit it.

Alejandro Jodorowsky

44.

Become obsessed with your goal, so consumed into your goal you will start to see every possibility to achieve it. You will only see solutions and what is possible to accomplish your goal.

45.

You cannot have a happy ending to an unhappy journey.

Abraham Hicks

45.

If happiness is your end goal, don't go through a lot of unhappy moments to reach just a single moment of happiness at the end. It doesn't make sense. Choose your experience wisely and enjoy the travel, not just the goal.

46.

Let him that would move the world, first move himself."

Socrates

46.

It was a lot easier to change the world around me rather than going the other way around and trying to change the world. My world is already changed because of me. I focused on pulling myself out of poverty and then was able to help those around me because of my personal success.

47.

The future belongs to those who believe in the beauty of their dreams.

Eleanor Roosevelt

47.

It was so beautiful to see a dreamer without legs running at the last Olympics, something that was unheard of before he dreamt it and it became a reality. Just go for your dreams; don't see any limitations.

48.

What I did you can also do.

Jesus

48.

You are powerful more than you can imagine. Go for it, test it, and you will be pleasantly surprised. No excuses!

49.

They may forget what you said, but they will never forget how you made them feel.

Carl Buechner

49.

Emotions and feelings are very important tools to get us closer to our goals and this is what we try to accomplish in the first place anyway. Feel better; everything we do is in order to feel better. So start by focusing on feeling better yourself and when you interact with others, make them feel better.

50.

Today, no matter where I'm going and no matter what I am doing, it is my dominant intent to see that which I am wanting to see.

Abraham Hicks

50.

You can create your own affirmation that is relevant to your goal. Find what fits for you verbally, visually, emotionally. I have a habit of putting sticky notes on my mirror when I shave in the morning. It's a wonderful tool to remind me throughout the day to stay on course to accomplish my goals.

51.

One can never consent to creep when one feels an impulse to soar.

Helen Keller

51.

Do not settle. Go for your dreams. That has been my philosophy and I am very well off with family, friends, joy, and accomplishments. Go for it!

52.

You can't afford to let your happiness depend on the behavior of another person.

Alan Cohen

52.

You always have to be the master of your destiny. Nobody else can make you or break you if you do not allow them.

53.

*When you are grateful --
when you can see what you
have -- you unlock blessings
to flow in your life.*

Suze Orman

53.

Every master throughout the ages repeatedly told us about being thankful. It's a wonderful tool and like a magnet you attract more blessings. I found that to be true in my life and for the lives of those around me. Thankful people attract more things to be thankful for. Resentful people attract more things to be resentful for. You choose!

54.

There is always something beautiful to be found if you look for it

White Eagle

54.

Diversity is the order of this universe and it is beautiful. Can you imagine if we all looked alike, how boring that would be? If we all had the same clothes, cars, homes, thoughts? Look for the beauty of the body, mind, and spirit, and you will always find it.

55.

If you're not thinking about a negative thought, your vibration is going to raise to its natural positive place.

Abraham Hicks

55.

When you find yourself becoming negative, bring yourself back by paying attention to your breath. In the present moment without negativity you will naturally raise to a positive upward spiral if you allow it.

56.

Big results require big ambitions.

James Cham

56.

Visualize unlimited potential in what you try to accomplish. As far as health, as far as winning a gold medal, as far as finances or anything else in your life. Think big. Big thinkers for their time took us to the moon.

57.

The most rewarding things you do in life are often the ones that look like they cannot be done.

Arnold Palmer

57.

When I was young, my high school teacher told me I would never go to college. It was satisfying to know that not only did I get into college, I got but an MBA and a PhD and became a professor at some of the best universities in Los Angeles. That has always fueled me and given me energy when I was told I could not do something. It worked for me. I hope it will work for you as well.

58.

The intuitive mind is a sacred gift and the rational mind is a faithful servant.

Albert Einstein

58.

Your ability to feel emotions through visualization is a gift no other animal on this planet has. Use it.

59.

The will to conquer is the first condition of victory.

Ferdinand Foch, Marshal of France

59.

Desire has an amazing ability to summon powers from the universe that will help us to accomplish our goals. Strong desires drastically improve our chances to get what we want.

60.

What you think and what you get always matches.

Abraham Hicks

60.

If you think you're right, you're right. If you think you're wrong, you're wrong. It always works.

To get more inspirational Quotes, tips and trainings signup at

www.FitnessHope.com

Made in the USA
Columbia, SC
09 May 2022

60161370R00088